GREAT CARS

GREAT CARS

A SENSATIONAL COLLECTION FROM CLASSICS TO THE MODERN GREATS

PaRragon

Bath · New York · Singapore · Hong Kong · Cologne · Delhi
Melbourne · Amsterdam · Johannesburg · Auckland · Shenzhen

First published by Parragon in 2011

Parragon
Queen Street House
4 Queen Street
Bath BA1 1HE, UK

Designed, produced, and packaged by
Stonecastle Graphics Limited

Text by Andrew Noakes
Designed by Paul Turner and Sue Pressley
Edited by Philip de Ste. Croix

ISBN 978-1-4454-2888-8

Printed in China

Page 1: Mercedes-Benz SLS AMG.

Page 2: Dodge Viper SRT-10.

Page 3: Customized 1957 Ford Fairlane.

Right: Porsche 356.

Contents

Introduction

Cars move us like no other invention. The motor car gave us the chance to travel independently like never before, to go farther and faster with fewer and fewer restrictions. The car gave us our freedom, and introduced change into our lives. It changed the way we work, the way we shop and play, and live. It forced us to change our roads and our towns, and in the process changed our environment. The motor car may not always have changed our world for the better, but for most of us living without it is simply unthinkable.

The best cars are not just tools for transporting people from one place to another. The finest of them—the great cars—have style and soul that elevate them from mere functional objects, turning them into technical, artistic, or sporting stars. Whether they are graceful or aggressive in style, simple or sophisticated in engineering, whether they had a long and successful life, a brief moment of glory, or were an ignominious failure, these are the cars that stir the enthusiast's soul.

These are the cars you will find on the pages that follow—from the pioneers of the earliest days that proved the car was viable, through the classic cars that have stood the test of time, to some of the fastest, most flamboyant, and most expensive machines of today. Some of the cars featured here were built for the masses, some for the select few. There are small cars, fast cars, and luxury limousines, technical innovators, and style icons. They are all different but each one has its own claim to glory in the annals of motoring history—and each one is, in its own way, a great car.

Right: Ferrari's Enzo of 2002 is, so far, the ultimate expression of the Maranello marque's combination of speed and style. This stunning supercar can accelerate to 60 mph (97 kph) in 3.1 seconds and can reach 100 mph (161 kph) in 6.6 seconds, with a top speed of 220 mph (354 kph).

A World of Classics

Right: Bugatti's 1932 Type 55 was the road-going version of the Type 51 Grand Prix car. The car's magnificent styling was by Ettore Bugatti's son Jean.

Below: The Type 35 is one of the best-known Bugattis, a two-seat racing car that dominated many races in the late 1920s. The engine was a 2.0-liter or 2.3-liter straight eight, available with supercharger or "unblown."

Opposite: W.O. Bentley built cars under his own name from 1919, concentrating on large and powerful machines, which contrasted with the lithe, jewel-like Bugattis of the same era. His first product was the 3-liter, powered by a four-cylinder engine with an overhead camshaft and four valves per cylinder—both highly unusual for their era. The 3-liter won at Le Mans in 1924 and 1927, then larger-engined Bentleys won in 1928, 1929, and 1930. However, in 1930 the Great Depression destroyed demand for the company's expensive products and it was eventually taken over by Rolls-Royce, which introduced a new range of cars.

Right: E.L. Cord bought the Duesenberg company in 1926 and gave the Duesenberg brothers a free hand to create the best car possible. The result was this, the Model J. Fitted with a 6.9-liter twin overhead camshaft engine with a claimed 265 hp, the Model J could thunder to 100 mph (161 kph) or more, making the servo-assisted hydraulic brakes essential. Introduced in 1929—just as the Great Depression hit the USA—the Model J was produced until 1937, by which time 435 of these extraordinary cars had been made. There was also an even faster supercharged version, the SJ.

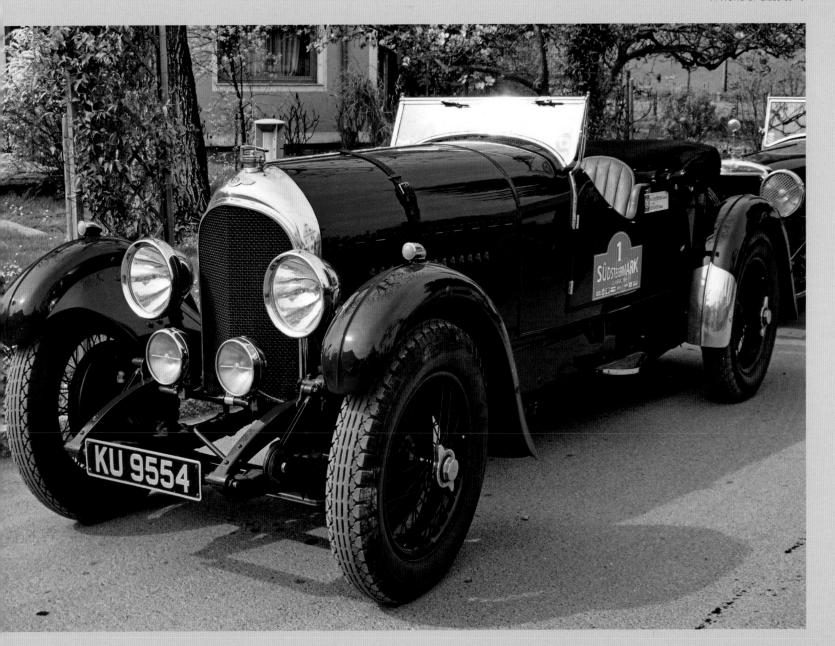

Opposite: Henry Ford pioneered the mass production of cars on a truly large scale with the Model T of 1908, but clung to the Model T concept for too long. When production finally came to an end in 1927, there was no successor in place. Ford factories lay idle for six months while this car, the Model A, was readied for production. This 1931 Model A has an unusual, but authentic, two-tone paint scheme.

Below: Like the Model T before it, the Model A was all things to all people—in this case a utilitarian pickup.

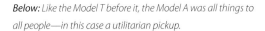

Above left: The Mini, brainchild of engineering genius Alec Issigonis, was an alternative to the 1950s bubble car. More than five million were built between 1959 and 2000.

Above: The Volkswagen Beetle was, literally, the "people's car" of Germany. The original idea came from Adolf Hitler, and the design was by the renowned Ferdinand Porsche.

Below: Before the Mini, the "baby" Austin A30 was the smallest proper car in the UK. This is the revised A35, with a stronger engine and other improvements, introduced in 1956.

Opposite: Citroën has always been a great innovator, though that has not always led the firm to financial success. The Traction Avant was a novel front-wheel-drive machine of monocoque construction, but the cost of its development bankrupted the company. André Citroën never saw the Traction Avant completed: he died of cancer in 1935, and the car did not go on sale until 1937.

Left: The DS was another innovative Citroën, with hydraulic suspension that provided a peerless ride. Like the Traction Avant, it sold well over a long production life.

Below: BMW's 328 sports car, introduced in 1936, combined a modern and very stiff twin-tube chassis and an innovative six-cylinder engine. Rudolf Schleicher, BMW's engine designer, wanted to use an efficient hemispherical combustion chamber with opposed valves for good engine breathing. Normally that would mean using expensive twin overhead camshafts, but instead Schleicher invented a "cross pushrod" system to operate all the valves from a single camshaft. The 328 became a very successful competition car, dominating sports car racing in the prewar years. This special coupé version won the shortened Mille Miglia in 1940.

Opposite: Ford's GT40 came into production after an attempt to buy Ferrari was vetoed by Enzo Ferrari at the last minute. Ford vowed to end Ferrari's domination of the Le Mans 24-hour race. After a troubled development program, the Fords finally won the race in 1966.

Right: Jaguar's D-type, introduced in 1954, had a low-drag body for high top speed and a lightweight, aircraft-inspired structure. Contaminated fuel slowed the D-types at Le Mans in its debut year of 1954, but it won the race in 1955, 1956, and 1957.

Above: The C-type Jaguar used the 3.4-liter twin-cam engine from the XK sports car in a lightweight tubular chassis. Jaguar won the Le Mans 24-hours with its C-type in 1951 and 1953, and might have won in 1952 but for an ill-conceived low-drag nose, which caused overheating.

Left: Rudolf Uhlenhaut conceived the Mercedes-Benz 300SL as a lightweight sports-racing car using largely existing Mercedes production car components, in a lightweight spaceframe chassis. The 300SL won the Le Mans race in 1952, the year the C-type Jaguars failed.

Opposite: MG courted controversy in 1955 by replacing the very traditional T-series cars with the much more modern MGA, but the new car was a huge sales success.

Left: Triumph's TR series of sports cars began with the TR2 in 1953. Full-width styling arrived with the TR4 of 1961. The TRs were classic open sports cars, and are still well loved today.

Below and right: Donald Healey's Healey Hundred sports car was produced by Austin as the Austin-Healey 100 (right). The larger-engined 3000 (below) was a successful rally car.

Opposite: Ferdinand Porsche was aged 72 when he started making cars under his own name in 1948 with the 356, which continued in production until 1965.

Left and below left: Mercedes-Benz introduced two sports cars in 1954. This one, the 190SL, was the mass-market model—but it looked very similar to the more expensive 300SL.

Below: The 300SL road car was descended directly from the racing car, which won at Le Mans in 1952 using a similar tubular spaceframe chassis and fuel-injected six-cylinder engine.

These pages: The tail fin era of automobile styling started in the 1950s and peaked between 1958 and 1960. It was a vogue that spread worldwide, as car designers picked up styling trends from the American automobile industry. General Motors' design chief Harley Earl is credited with the automobile tail fin, introducing small fins on the 1948 Cadillac. Taking the appearance of World War II fighter aircraft as his inspiration, Earl's tail fin assemblies (including tail lights) were designed increasingly to resemble the tail fins of contemporary jet fighters and space rockets. Combining polished chrome and brightly painted bodywork completed the style of the period.

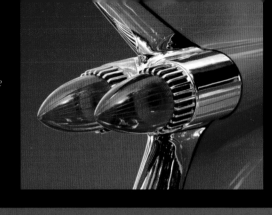

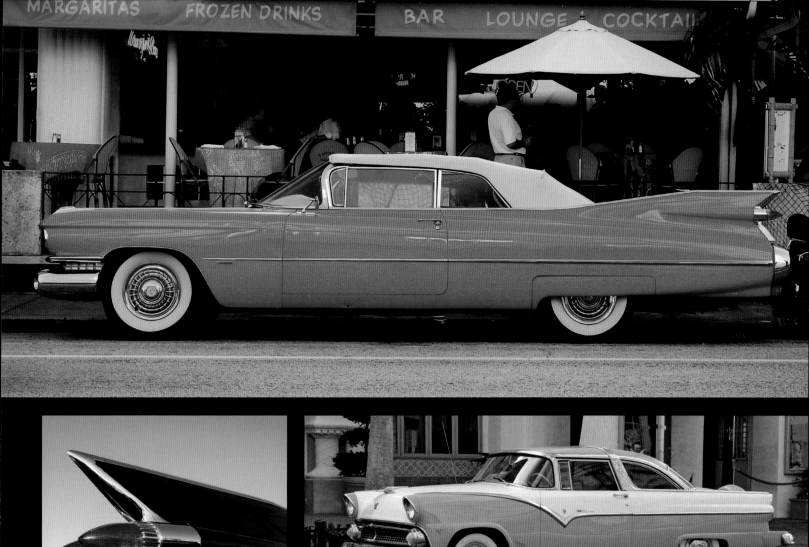

Power and Performance

Right: Jaguar stunned the motoring world when the E-type was introduced in 1961. In 1971 the car was given a new engine, a 5.3-liter V12. The car pictured is one of the very last E-types, built in 1975.

Below: The E-type was available both as an open roadster and, as here, a fastback coupé. There were two fixed-roof cars—a two-seater and a 2+2 with a higher roofline.

Opposite: Two generations of the Jaguar XK meet at the base of the London Eye. The XK120 (right) was Jaguar's first postwar sports car, and the fastest production car of its time—yet on its introduction in 1948 it was offered for a remarkably low price. This particular example, carrying the registration NUB 120, won the first ever Alpine Rally Gold Cup, awarded for a penalty-free run. The latest XK (left) is an accomplished V8-engined GT car with an appealing blend of performance and refinement, available both as a roadster and a coupé.

Above and right: *The Dodge Viper could only have come from the United States. Enormous for a sports car, and powered by a V10 engine that originally saw service in a light truck, it was the antithesis of the lightweight, nimble, European ideal.*

Left: *AC's Ace provided the basic chassis and bodywork, which, combined with a Ford V8 engine, produced by the Anglo-American Cobra, has since spawned numerous copycats. The original Cobra was conceived by US race driver and engineer Carroll Shelby.*

This page: America's original, and possibly best-known, sports car is the iconic Chevrolet Corvette, which has developed through six generations since its introduction in 1953. The sixth-generation C6 Corvette was introduced in 2005, and in 2009 a high-performance ZR1 model was added to the range. It is powered by a 6.2-liter LS9 V8 engine fitted with a four-lobe Eaton supercharger, which boosts output to 638 bhp. As a result the ZR1 scorches to 60 mph (97 kph) from rest in 3.3 seconds and can power on to a top speed of 205 mph (330 kph). It is also said to generate 1.1 g of lateral acceleration in cornering—a very high figure.

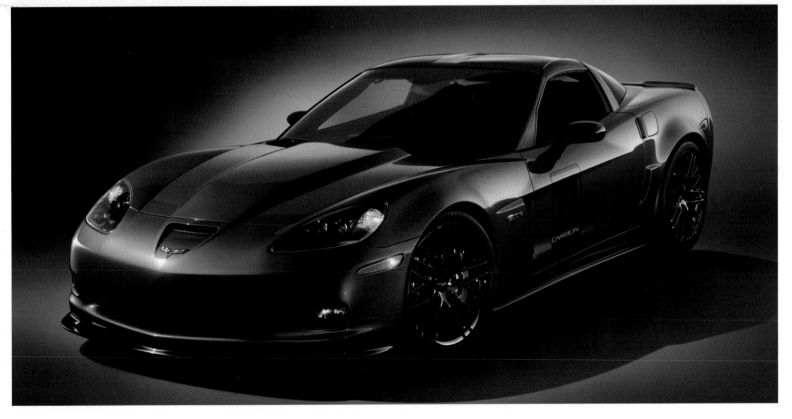

These pages: Aston Martin has produced some of the world's most sought-after cars since its inception in 1913. One of the most influential was the DB4GT Zagato of the 1960s (above), a lightweight racing sports car. Traditional Aston Martin styling elements such as the grille shape and the front wing side vents, and cues from the Zagato such as the "haunched" shape of the rear wings, are still seen in Astons today. The V8 Vantage (opposite), DB9 (right), and DBS Volante (far right) are examples of today's Astons. They have received widespread critical acclaim for their styling and performance.

Left: The Roadmaster was at the top of the Buick range in the 1950s—powerful, well-appointed, and laden with chrome. A four-door sedan and two-door convertible were also available.

Right: In the 1960s American cars switched their emphasis from luxury to power. This is one of the first of this era of "muscle cars," the 1964 Pontiac GTO.

Below: The second generation GTO continued the power theme, but before long muscle cars were emasculated in the wake of safety and emissions concerns.

Above: In recent years the muscle car has seen a revival, with modern versions of classic shapes. This is the 2010 Dodge Challenger in two guises—R/T Classic (left) and SE Rallye (right).

Left: The "Bumble Bee" Chevrolet Camaro was specially built for the Transformers film. It was based on the 2006 Chevrolet Camaro concept car.

Right: The production version of the latest Chevrolet Camaro was introduced in 2010. It recalls the styling of the original Camaro, built from 1967 to 1969.

Opposite: The F430 was Ferrari's mid-engined V8 sports car offering from 2004 to 2009.

Right: The 308GTB was Ferrari's first mid-engined V8 two-seater, introduced in 1975.

Far right: The Ferrari 360 Challenge Stradale was a lighter, track-focused version of the 360 Modena.

Below: In 2010 Ferrari introduced its latest mid-engined car, the 458 Italia—seen here at the Goodwood Festival of Speed.

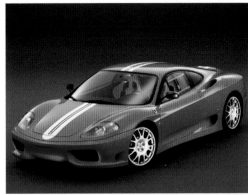

Top: BMW's Z4 was one of a growing range of modern sports cars that featured a folding roof.

Above: The Mazda MX-5 was one of the first modern roadsters. This is the third-generation model.

Right: Porsche's two-seater Boxster had much in common with the larger, faster, and more expensive 911.

Opposite: Like many roadsters, the Honda S2000 was available with an optional hardtop for winter weather.

Above: Subaru's World Rally contenders were built by the Prodrive team in Banbury, UK. They were based on the road-going Impreza Turbo.

Right: Though not as quick as the competition cars, the road-going turbocharged Impreza WRX and STi models were fast and responsive.

Far right: The Lancia Delta Integrale was a rally-inspired car from an earlier era. It won the World Rally Championship constructor's title six times between 1987 and 1992.

Right: Audi's quattro coupé, introduced at the Geneva motor show in 1980, was the first practical four-wheel-drive rally car and revolutionized the sport. The quattro was also a rapid, sure-footed road car. Production continued until 1991, and quattro four-wheel-drive models are still part of Audi's range today.

Above and right: John Cooper developed the original Mini into a pocket-sized performance car, and it had a long and successful career in rallying. BMW's new Mini still has Cooper-badged models (above), and in 2011 it will enter the World Rally Championship with a four-wheel-drive car based on the Mini Countryman (right).

Above: The Mercedes-Benz CLK-GTR was built for new sports car racing regulations in 1997. Just 25 production cars were made, and at the time it was the most expensive car on sale, with a price of more than $1.5 million. It had a 6.8-liter V12 engine and a top speed of 215 mph (346 kph).

Right and far right: Aston Martin's entry in the GT1 racing class was the DBR9, unveiled in 2005. It won its class in the Le Mans 24-hour race in 2007 and 2008. The DBR9 is powered by a V12 engine derived from Aston's road-car unit.

Right: Porsche's GT3 models were track-focused, with tuned normally aspirated engines and more extreme aerodynamic aids. The GT3 version of the 997, announced in 2006, produced 429 bhp and could accelerate from 60 mph (0–97 kph) in 4.1 seconds. It had a top speed of 190 mph (306 kph).

Below: The Porsche Carrera GT was a V10-powered supercar unveiled in 2004. It was originally intended as a racing car, but the project was canceled. It was later revived as a limited-production road car. The 605 bhp 5.7-liter engine gave it a top speed of 205 mph (330 kph).

Left: Britain has a long history of niche sports car makers. None has had a more checkered career than TVR, which was founded by Trevor Wilkinson in 1946. Introduced in 1996, the Cerbera marked the first use of TVR's own "AJP" engines, designed by Al Melling. Production of the Cerbera continued until 2003.

Below: The Blackpool-based TVR company survived through a number of owners until 2006, when production ended. The Sagaris was one of the company's final products, and was fitted with TVR's own Speed Six engine—a 4.0-liter straight six developing 380 bhp, good for a 185 mph (298 kph) top speed.

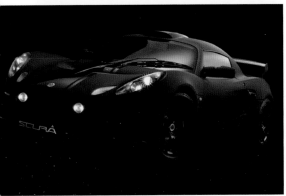

Above: Lotus's successful mid-engined roadster, the Elise, was the spiritual successor to the no-frills Lotus Seven of the 1950s. The Elise S, shown here, had a top speed of 127 mph (204 kph).

Left: Lotus has based most of its recent cars on the Elise, unveiled in 1996. This is the high-performance Exige Scura, with a supercharged 257 bhp engine and matte-black paint.

Right: Lee Noble founded his company in 1999. Though he has now left to pursue other projects, Noble Automotive continues. Its latest car is the twin-turbocharged 650 bhp M600.

Left: Japanese marques have produced some of the most amazing performance cars of recent years. This is the Nissan GTR, unveiled in 2007.

Right: Nissan's 350Z was a more affordable sports car. This curvaceous car is fitted with Nismo (Nissan Motorsport) tuning and styling components.

Below: Honda's NSX, introduced in 1990, was the first true supercar from a Japanese manufacturer. F1 champion Ayrton Senna was involved in its development.

Left and below: Lexus began work on the LFA supercar in 2000, but production did not begin until 2010. The LFA is unusual because of its extensive use of carbon fiber composites in the chassis and bodywork. Yamaha helped develop the 4.8-liter V10 engine, which has a 9,000 rpm rev limit and delivers 552 bhp to the rear wheels through a six-speed sequential automatic transmission. Just 500 LFAs will be built, and the last of them is expected to be delivered in 2012. By then, the roadster, shown below in concept form at the Detroit show in 2008, might be a production reality.

Right: The Alfa Romeo 8C Competizione has supercar DNA: its engine is the same V8 unit used by both Ferrari and Maserati. First seen in concept form in 2003, the 8C went into production in 2007. Just 500 were built, making this one of the rarest Alfas of recent times.

Below: The Alfa TZ3, unveiled in 2010, celebrated the 90th anniversary of the partnership between Alfa Romeo and the coach-builder Zagato. A one-off commissioned by a wealthy Alfa enthusiast, the TZ3 is powered by the 8C Competizione's 4.7-liter V8 engine.

Left: Horacio Pagani unveiled his Zonda C12 supercar in 1999. Early cars used a 6.0-liter Mercedes-Benz V12 engine, but recent Paganis have upgraded to a 7.3-liter V12. The unique Zonda Tricolore seen here celebrates the 50th anniversary of the Frecce Tricolore, the Italian aerobatic display team.

Below: Since 1999 Maserati has been under the control of its long-time rival Ferrari. The first Maserati of the modern era was the 3200GT, followed by the Coupé and Spyder and then the GranTurismo, seen here, from 2007. Maserati also produced the MC12 and the Quattroporte luxury sedan.

Left: Lamborghini was another Italian marque to be reborn under new owners. Audi has owned the company since 1998, and in 2001 introduced this flagship model, the Murciélago. It was styled by the Belgian designer Luc Donckerwolke and powered by a 6.2-liter V12 engine developing 572 bhp. More powerful versions followed, together with a smaller and cheaper sister model, the Gallardo, and the limited-edition Reventón. More than 4,000 Murciélagos have been built, but production is expected to end in 2011. The Murciélago will be replaced in 2012 by a new flagship model, the Jota.

Right: The tiny British Morgan Car Company makes cars that combine traditional style and craftsmanship with modern engineering and performance. The Aero 8 introduced in 2001 had controversial styling, but there was no doubt about the performance provided by the 4.4-liter BMW powerplant.

Below: BMW established a new factory at Goodwood to build a new range of Rolls-Royce cars from 2003. The first model was the Phantom sedan, and this provided the basis for the 2007 Phantom Drophead. The Drophead's styling was first seen on the 100EX concept car in 2004.

Left: *Maserati followed up the launch of the GranTurismo coupé in 2007 with this, the GranCabrio, in 2009. It was powered by a 4.7-liter V8 engine, which like the "S" version of the coupé, developed 434 bhp. Power was delivered to the rear wheels through a six-speed ZF automatic gearbox.*

Below: *BMW's 6-series convertible, known internally as the E64, was available with a choice of gasoline and diesel engines. The M6 version shared a 500 bhp V10 engine with the M5 sedan. A new-generation F13 6-series convertible was due to go on sale in 2011.*

Right: Ford design chief J. Mays described the reinvention of car designs from the past as "retro futurism." The 2005 Ford Mustang demonstrated the point, using styling "cues" from the 1960s Mustang but bringing them up to date. This is the Boss 302, the most powerful Mustang ever.

Below: Clearly inspired by the Ford GT40 of the 1960s, but very different in detail, the Ford GT was a supercar to be used on the roads rather than a racer. It featured an aluminum structure and a supercharged 5.4-liter V8 engine. Just over 4,000 were built in 2005 and 2006.

Opposite: The Mercedes-Benz SLS AMG, unveiled in 2009, brought back the "gullwing" doors that had been such a recognizable feature of the original Mercedes SL in 1952. The SLS was chosen as the official Formula 1 Safety Car for the 2010 season.

Below: In 2009 Alan Lubinsky of AC Cars announced the AC MkVI, which was to be built in Germany by Gullwing GmbH. Though the styling was clearly similar to the ACs of yesteryear, the new car used an "aluminum hybrid" body, modern Corvette V8 engine, and Porsche brakes.

Opposite: Ferrari's Enzo supercar of 2002 brought F1 technology to the road, including the use of carbon fiber bodywork and a carbon/aluminum chassis.

Right: A Ferrari from an earlier age, the unusually styled 250GT "breadvan" was based on a 1961 Ferrari 250GT SWB. Giotto Bizzarrini designed the low-drag body.

Below: The 599GTO, Ferrari's new limited-edition V12 Berlinetta, is a track-focused development of the 599GTB, seen here on the Goodwood House hillclimb course.

Modern Greats

Right: McLaren launched the MP4-12C late in 2009—its first road car since the legendary F1. It has a carbon composite chassis, a bespoke 3.8-liter, twin-turbo V8 engine, and a seven-speed dual-clutch gearbox.

Below: Jaguar's XKR, seen here in convertible form, is one of a growing number of modern high performance cars to use a supercharged engine.

Above: *Porsche's 911 Turbo, of the latest 997 generation, is one of the most usable supercars of all. Launched in 2006, it features a 470 bhp flat-six engine with twin variable geometry turbochargers—a first for a gasoline-powered car. A convertible version went on sale in 2007.*

Right and far right: *Audi's four-wheel-drive, V10-engined R8 (far right) challenged Porsche's dominance of the "practical supercar" market. Tuning company ABT turned it into a lighter, more powerful, and more focused driving machine, which they called the R8 GT R (right).*

Opposite: Aston Martin's Vanquish S was the last car built at the famous Newport Pagnell factory in the UK, but Astons continue to be made at Gaydon, Warwickshire.

Left: The Mercedes-Benz SL65AMG Black Series boasts 661 bhp from its hand-built, twin-turbo V12 engine. Its top speed is limited to 199 mph (320 kph).

Below: Bentley's Continental Supersports was its fastest road car ever, with more power (621 bhp) and less weight than the standard Continental.

Above and right: Aston Martin's One-77 boasted the most powerful normally aspirated engine of any road car—a mammoth 7.3-liter V12 delivering 750 bhp. The top speed exceeds 220 mph (354 kph). The One-77 has a carbon monocoque structure with aluminum alloy exterior panels. Just 77 production cars will be built—hence the car's name— priced at well over $1.4 million each.

Left and below: Just five examples of the Pagani Zonda Cinque, and five more of the Cinque Roadster seen here, will be produced. Both feature magnesium and titanium suspension components, a new sequential manual transmission, and a revised 678 bhp engine.

Left and below: *Dutch car maker Spyker builds bespoke sports cars in small numbers for a select clientele. The company's first car was the C8, fitted with a 4.2-liter Audi V8 engine developing 394 bhp. In 2009 Spyker announced that it was moving its production line to Coventry, in the UK.*

Left: *The Spyker C12 Zagato, announced at the Geneva show in 2007, was styled by the famous Italian styling house of Zagato. As with other Spyker models, power comes from an Audi engine, this time a 6.0-liter W12 producing 500 bhp. The top speed is said to be 193 mph (310 kph), and 0– 60 mph (97 kph) acceleration takes just 3.8 seconds.*

Right and below: The Gallardo was Lamborghini's second new model under Audi ownership, launched in 2003. Unlike its big brother, the V12-engined Murciélago, the Gallardo was powered by a 5.0-liter V10 engine. In its original form this generated 493 bhp, and a detuned version was later used in Audi's own R8. The Gallardo was available with a conventional manual gearbox or a robotized transmission that Lamborghini called "E-gear." The LP560-4 (in Spyder convertible form, right) featured a 552 bhp 5.2-liter engine, producing a top speed of around 200 mph (322 kph), and revised E-gear transmission. It was introduced in 2008.

Left: Lotus expanded its range beyond its Elise-based cars with the Evora of 2008. Unusual because of its mid-engined two-plus-two configuration, the Evora is powered by a 3.5-liter Toyota V6 engine. With 276 bhp on tap, it can achieve 162 mph (260 kph).

Below: The Porsche Cayman is a mid-engined two-seater coupé based on the Boxster roadster. Porsche specialist Robert Sikkens Racing created this Cayman GT to show off some of its tuning options for the car—including a 550 bhp twin-turbo engine, sports suspension, a revised exhaust system, and new aerodynamic aids.

Right: BMW's M3 proves that a practical sedan can still be a very fast car. The latest generation M3 has a 4.0-liter V8 engine providing a top speed of 155 mph (250 kph). Manual and dual-clutch gearboxes are offered. The coupé, shown here, has a carbon composite roof to save weight.

Below: The M5 is BMW's big performance sedan. Production of the E60 generation M5 shown here came to an end in 2010 after 20,000 had been built. It will be the last M5 powered by a large, normally aspirated engine—in this case a 5.0-liter V10, which developed a peak output of 507 bhp.

This page: Cadillac launched its CTS-V coupé at the Detroit motor show early in 2010. It packed the same 548 bhp punch as the CTS-V sedan, from a 6.2-liter supercharged V8 engine, which had also seen service in the Corvette ZR1. The result was an extraordinarily rapid car, able to sprint from rest to 60 mph (97 kph) in less than 4 seconds and go on to a top speed of 185 mph (298 kph). The sedan lapped the Nürburgring race circuit in less than eight minutes, and GM claimed that it was the fastest production sedan in the world.

Right: These are some of the fastest cars the world has ever seen. McLaren's F1, launched in 1993, held the title of fastest production car for more than ten years. It achieved 231 mph (372 kph) in standard form, and 243 mph (391 kph) with the rev-limiter disabled.

Below: The 987 bhp Bugatti Veyron took the fastest production car record in 2005, achieving 253 mph (407 kph) at VW's Ehra-Lessien test track. SSC broke the record in 2007, but in 2010 the 1,184 bhp Veyron Super Sport recaptured it for Bugatti, at 268 mph (431 kph).

Left: The Koenigsegg CCR was the fastest production car in the world for a few months in 2005, before the Bugatti Veyron arrived on the scene. The CCR was replaced by the CCX, which was powered by a Ford-based twin-turbocharged V8 engine of 4.7 liters, developing 806 bhp.

Below: The car that beat the Veyron's top speed was the SSC Ultimate Aero, which achieved 256 mph (412 kph) on a closed road in Washington State in 2007. The Ultimate Aero had a 6.35-liter V8 engine with twin turbochargers, developing 1,183 bhp. It has a composite body and tubular steel frame.

Right: The Lotus Esprit was one of six new Lotus models announced at the Paris motor show in 2010. It has a 5.0-liter V8 engine and optional KERS (Kinetic Energy Recovery System) hybrid technology.

Below: BMW's Vision EfficientDynamics made its debut at the Frankfurt show in 2009. Showing a way forward for BMW's performance cars, the Vision was propelled by a diesel-electric hybrid powertrain using a 1.5-liter, three-cylinder turbodiesel engine and two electric motors—which between them produced 351 bhp.

Right: Jaguar's C-X75 was one of the surprises of the 2010 Paris salon, and for many people the star of the show. The striking supercar shape has all the glamor and animal muscularity of the best Jaguars, with hints of the 1950s D-type and the unraced 1960s XJ13. The drivetrain is as exciting as it is modern—the C-X75 has four 195 bhp electric motors and a pair of tiny gas turbines, which spin at up to 80,000 rpm. Jaguar claim a top speed of 205 mph (330 kph) and a 0–62 mph (100 kph) sprint time of just 3.4 seconds.

Left: Ferrari's SA Aperta is a roadster development of the 599, built to celebrate the 80th anniversary of Ferrari's long-time design partner Pininfarina. Only 80 will be built—and every one was sold before the car was even officially unveiled.

Below: The GTbyCitroën concept was a collaboration between Citroën and computer game company Polyphony, and featured in the Playstation driving simulation Gran Turismo 5. The car's outlandish looks were said to reduce lift and drag to improve its dynamics at high speed. Rumors suggested that it would feature an American V8 engine and paddle-shift gearbox.

Index

Picture credits

a = above, b = below, l = left, r = right, c = center

© Manufacturers' Press Pictures: AC Cars 46(br); Alfa Romeo Automobiles 42(a); Aston Martin Lagonda Ltd 26, 36(br), 54(al), 54(ar); Audi AG 51(bl), 51(br); BMW Group AG 32(al), 45(b), 58, 62(bl); Bugatti 8(a); Chrysler/Dodge 24(a), 24(br), 29(a); Ferrari S.p.A. 31(ar), 63(a); Ford Motor Company 14, 46(a); General Motors/Buick 28(al); General Motors/ Cadillac 59; General Motors/Chevrolet 25, 29(br); General Motors/Pontiac 28(ar); Honda Motor Company 33, 40(b); Jaguar Cars Ltd 15(a), 15(br), 22–23, 50(b), 62(br); Koenigsegg Automotive AB 61(a); Automobili Lamborghini S.p.A. 43(bl), 56(a); Lancia Automobiles S.p.A. 34(br); Lexus 41; Lotus Cars 39(a), 39(bl), 57(a), 62(a); Maserati 43(br), 45(a); Mazda Motor Corporation 32(bl); McLaren Automotive 50(a); Mercedes-Benz/Daimler AG 1, 15(bl), 19, 36(a), 47, 53(ar); Mini 11 (al); Mini/BMW Group AG 35(bl), 35(br); Morgan Car Company 44(a); Nissan Motor Company 40(al), 40(ar); Noble Automotive 39(br); Pagani Automobili S.p.A. 43(a), 54(bl), 54(br); Porsche AG 37(b); Rolls-Royce Motor Cars Ltd 44(b); Shelby 24(bl); Spyker Cars N.V. 55; SSC (Shelby Super Cars), Inc. 61(bl); Subaru 34(bl); TVR 38(a); Volkswagen 11(ar).

© magiccarpics.co.uk: 38(b), 60(a).

© Shutterstock.com: 20(b), 46(bl); Bianca Lagalla 21(a); Carlos Arguelles 20(ar); corepics 13(a); DeepGreen 9; Dmitriy Bryndin 29(bl); Fedor Selivanov 12; hfng 2; Igor Plotnikov 16; Ivan Cholakov Gostock-dot-net 21(br); jon le-bon 11(br); KENCKOphotography 13(b); Maksim Toome 56(b); Marafona 11(bl); Max Earey 4-5, 18, 27, 31(b), 32(r), 34(a), 36(bl), 37(a), 42(b), 49(b), 51(a), 52, 53(b), 57(b), 60(b), 63(b); Michael Shake 10; Michael Stokes 49(a); oksana.perkins 6–7, 30, 48; Olga Lis 20(al); pasphotography 28(br); Paul Matthew Photography 21(bl); Philip Lange 17(b); photoBeard 17(ar); Stuart Elflett 17(al); ttueni 3.

Creative Commons License: Berlin 13407 31(al); Bildmachine 8(bl); Brian Snelson 35(a); Magnus Bäck 8(br).

The author and publishers have made every reasonable effort to credit all copyright holders. Any errors or omissions that may have occurred are inadvertent and anyone who for any reason has not been credited is invited to write to the publishers so that a full acknowledgment may be made in subsequent editions of this work.